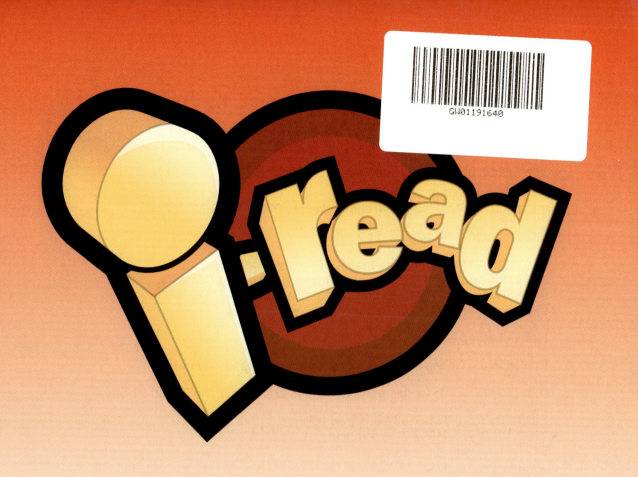

Non-fiction 3

Series editor: Pie Corbett

CAMBRIDGE
UNIVERSITY PRESS

CAMBRIDGE UNIVERSITY PRESS
Cambridge, New York, Melbourne, Madrid, Cape Town, Singapore, São Paulo

Cambridge University Press
The Edinburgh Building, Cambridge CB2 2RU, UK

www.cambridge.org
Information on this title: www.cambridge.org/9780521618823

© Cambridge University Press 2005

This book is in copyright. Subject to statutory exception
and to the provisions of relevant collective licensing agreements,
no reproduction of any part may take place without
the written permission of Cambridge University Press.

First published 2005

Printed in the United Kingdom at the University Press, Cambridge

A catalogue record for this publication is available from the British Library

ISBN-13 978-0-521-61882-3 paperback
ISBN-10 0-521-61882-7 paperback

Acknowledgements

Cover
© Rob Howard/CORBIS

Photos
p.8 Johann de Meester, Ardea.com; p.32 S&R Greenhill; p.33 Action Sports; p.34 Beach Feature.com; p.35 Claus Lunau, Bonnier Publications, Science Photo Library; p. 36 Ingraham Image Libary 500 Volume 2

Artwork
Beehive Illustration (Mark Turner, Pulsar, Sandeep Kaushik)

Texts
All texts by Ann Webley

Contents

Non-chronological reports by Ann Webley   5

A Rather Different Pet   6
Keeping a Ferret as a Pet   8
Keeping a Cockatoo as a Pet   11
Keeping a Ball Python as a Pet   14
Keeping a Stick Insect as a Pet   17

Instructions by Ann Webley   21

Sam's Hobby Club   22
Hopscotch   24
How to Find the Goblin's Gold   26
How to Snare the Dragon   28

Alphabetical texts by Ann Webley   31

An ABC of Getting About   32

Letters by Ann Webley   37

Letter from Mr Gruff to Mrs Washer   38
Letter from Jack to Jill   40
Letter from Henny Penny to Jack   42
Letter from Contrary Mary to Jack Washer   44
Extracts from four letters   46
An Invitation to the Ball   48
Letter from Loolabell Hardup to Mistress Simkins   50
Letter from Cinders to Buttons   52
Letter from the Lord Chamberlain   54

Non-chronological reports

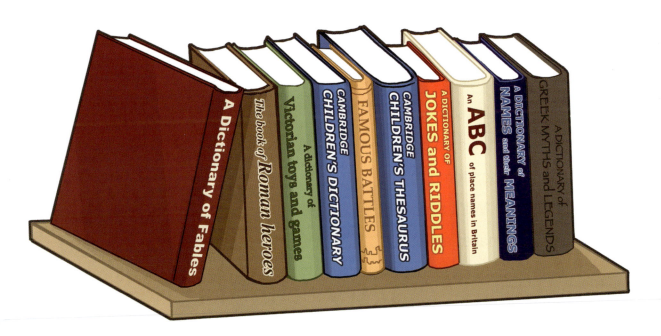

A Rather Different Pet

"I want a pet, Mum," Fraser announced when he got home from school on Friday. "Sam's got one – a new puppy. He's really cute."

Mrs Watson sighed. "Now, Fraser," she said, "we've been through this before. It's not fair to have a puppy when everyone is out all day."

"I know that," Fraser said. "I don't want a puppy."

Mrs Watson thought for a bit. "Let's go down to the pet shop tomorrow," she said. "We'll see what sort of smaller animals they've got that would be happy in our flat. What do you think of that?"

Fraser beamed. "Oh, yes, please! That will be great!"

The next day, Mr Bowen showed them a lot

of different animals. Fraser wasn't interested in the rabbits, the hamsters, the gerbils or the mice. He wanted something different.

"I'll tell you what," Mr Bowen said. "Why don't you try to find out about some other pets from books or the Internet and see if they'd be happy in your flat?"

So Fraser did.

Keeping a Ferret as a Pet

A ferret is a small animal that is now a popular pet. Ferrets live for about eight years.

Appearance

Ferrets are around forty centimetres long. They have long, thin bodies and short legs. Many are brown but some are 'albino'. These are white with pink eyes. There are also lots of other colours to choose from.

Habitat

The ferret will need a large wire cage. This should be a multi-storey one so that your pet can explore. Make sure that the wire has small holes or your ferret could hurt itself. You need to put some objects in the cage to keep the ferret happy.

Ferrets like to swing on hammocks, play with toys and crawl in tubes. A ferret can also be trained to use a litter tray like a cat. The ferret will want soft bedding of something like wood shavings. Do not forget to clean the cage out once a week. It is better if the cage is not in the sunlight or where the animal can get cold.

Food

You can give your ferret 'dry complete ferret food'. This is good because it contains all the goodness your pet needs. Ferrets also like some minced meat, liver or eggs as a treat.

What they do

Ferrets are very friendly and clever. They sleep for 15–18 hours a day but when they are awake they need lots of playtime. Two ferrets love to play together. They need to play with humans as well.

1. Ferrets are always exploring and they will collect and hide objects. Maybe this is why their name means 'little thief' in Latin! Make sure that your ferret cannot escape before you let it out into a room. The family needs to be able to put up with all the things the ferret will do, such as hiding socks and car keys or unrolling toilet paper all over the house!

2. You will see your ferret do the 'dance of joy'. It will jump from side to side, flip on the floor and bounce off the furniture. It will look as if it has gone mad! It may make chirping noises. This means that your ferret is very happy indeed.

3 Ferrets 'talk' by making funny little noises. Sometimes they will bite. They will do this to get attention and also to show they are cross. Ferrets do not like being woken up and they may bite if this happens.

Other information

Ferrets are not difficult to look after. They need baths often. After they have had a bath, you can brush their fur with a soft brush. They will shed their coats twice a year. Clean their outer ears with a cotton bud but be careful not to poke it inside. Ferrets need to have their nails cut every 2–3 weeks. They will make a big fuss about this!

It is important to think carefully before you choose a ferret as a pet. Ferrets need a lot of time spent on them but they are a lot of fun because they are so friendly and easy to tame.

Keeping a Cockatoo as a Pet

Cockatoos are large members of the parrot family. They can live for more than forty years and they make very good pets.

Appearance

Cockatoos can be many different colours. They all have a crest on their head. The birds will often show the mood they are in with their crest. If the crest is standing straight up, they feel excited. If it is moving up and down or sliding back, they feel scared. Cockatoos grow to a length of 30–45 cm.

Habitat

Your cockatoo will need a big cage that is some way above the floor. The size of the cage will depend on the size of the bird. The cockatoo must be able to spread its wings inside it.

Most cages are about one metre long, one metre wide and one metre high. The cage must also have good locks on the door. Cockatoos have strong beaks and they will try to get out! The bars of the cage must be quite close together so that the bird cannot get trapped. Cockatoos do not like to be too hot or too cold and they must be out of draughts. Put some toys into the cage for the cockatoo to bite and chew on. The bird will get bored with them after a time, just like you do with your toys. Find some new ones and your pet will be happy again! There should also be some perches. The cockatoo will stand on them to exercise its feet. It also needs some lukewarm water every few days to bathe in.

Food

Cockatoos are easy to feed. There is a 'parrot mixture' that will keep them fit and well. They also enjoy fresh fruit and vegetables. Do not give your cockatoo fruit seeds or chocolate because this will harm it. Cockatoos need to have fresh water every day. It is a good idea to put the food and water containers away from the perches so they do not get full of droppings!

What they do

Cockatoos are very friendly and need to be treated as one of the family. They need a lot of attention and playtime. They need time out of the cage and they like to be held. They will be happy to sit on someone's knee and be stroked. It is a good idea to take the bird out of the cage at the same time each day. It gets used to this. If you don't, the bird will scream until it is let out and that might not be very popular with the family! A cockatoo that is left on its own for too long will become ill. It might scream and pluck at its feathers to show that it is upset. Try to buy a young bird that is about three months old. It will get used to you and is much more likely to talk. Most will only say a few words or phrases. The Moluccan Cockatoo is very tame and friendly and talks more than others. Cockatoos that do talk have very clear voices and are sometimes very funny.

It is fun to look after birds like these which come from countries a long way away.

Keeping a Ball Python as a Pet

Snakes are **reptiles** that are becoming popular pets and many people keep Ball Pythons at home. These snakes have this name because of what they do when they are nervous. They make themselves into a tight ball with their head pulled in.

Appearance

A Ball Python is a fairly small snake. The adults grow to a length of **4–6 feet**. They can be gold and brown, dark green or black. They often have a black stripe with gold-brown spots down their back.

Habitat

All snakes are 'escape artists' and so they need somewhere to live that they cannot get out of. A snake should have a large tank so that it has lots of room to stretch. Put soil and moss or paper towels on the bottom. The snake must also have a hiding place such as a box or a hollow log. This needs to be just big enough for the snake to get in. Ball Pythons like warm homes. The temperature must be more than

21°C. It is best if the home is in sunlight. If this is not possible, you will need to buy sunlight bulbs. There must also be a very hot place where the snake can **bask** like it does in the wild. The tank will need a heating lamp for that part of the Ball Python's home.

The Ball Python's home needs a few objects to keep its occupant happy. First of all the snake needs water to soak in. Put this in a heavy bowl that cannot be knocked over. Change the water every day and clean the home once a week. In addition, put objects in the cage that your pet can explore. For example, it will like branches, ropes and shelves that hang down from the roof.

Food

Ball Pythons eat small rodents such as mice and rats. It is better to feed your snake dead animals because a live rat or mouse might hurt it. A lot of people keep the food in the freezer. They take it out when they want to feed the snake and let it warm up so it is the same as normal food. Young snakes eat once or twice a week. Adult snakes only eat every two weeks. Your pet will eat what it wants at once. Take out any food that is left.

Other information

The Ball Python is **nocturnal**. It will explore its home and hang from the ropes and branches. It will also stay still in the hide box for a long time. You can pick up your Ball Python and handle it gently. It is a good idea to do this each day so that it trusts you. Be careful because it could slither off! Like all snakes, the Ball Python will shed its skin. You will know when this is going to happen. Its eyes will turn light blue over a few days and its body colour will get duller. The snake will shed its skin in one piece and it is very interesting to watch.

Your friends will all love to watch your very different pet!

bask – *sit or lie in the sun without doing anything else*
4–6 feet – *1.5–2 metres*
nocturnal – *active at night and asleep in the day*
reptiles – *cold-blooded animals with a backbone and dry, scaly skin*

Keeping a Stick Insect as a Pet

There are many different kinds of **Phasmids** or stick insects and they are found in hot countries all over the world. They are now very popular pets. They live for about a year.

Appearance

Stick insects have an unusual appearance. Some people call them 'walking sticks' because of their shape. They hang from a leaf and put their front legs in front of their head. This is very good **camouflage** because it makes them look like part of the plant. When stick insects move, they sway from side to side so it looks as if they are being blown by the wind.

Habitat

A stick insect needs a tall tank containing lots of plants to live in. The tank needs mesh sides so the stick insect can cling on. Stick insects like heat and prefer the room to be around 24–27°C. If the room is

colder, you can use an electric light bulb to warm up the tank. It is a good idea to mist the plants' leaves with a spray bottle if you keep certain types of stick insect. This helps to keep the area like the stick insect's habitat in the wild. Some insects need an open bowl to drink out of. Do not worry if your stick insect leaves its head under water because it does not breathe through its mouth.

Food

Stick insects are **herbivores**. They have very powerful jaws and gnaw leaves with their small teeth. Different kinds of stick insects have different favourite leaves. The most common ones are privet and blackberry. It is amazing to think that such small insects can manage the leaves of plants like this.

What they do

Here are some of the things that stick insects do.

1. Stick insects **moult** and you will enjoy watching this happen. They hang upside down from the food plant and shed their skin. It is important to make sure that the tank is deep enough to let them hang. They usually eat the skin after they have moulted because it contains lots of goodness.

2. Stick insects have different ways of defending themselves in the wild. For example, they will change their body shape and colour so that they look like the plant they are living on. It is fun trying to spot them!

3. If stick insects are disturbed, they sometimes just drop to the ground and pretend to be dead.

Stick insects are not difficult to look after and you will find them very interesting pets.

camouflage – *colour or shape that makes an animal look the same as the things around it*

herbivores – *plant eaters*

moult – *lose skin and get another one*

Phasmids – *the scientific name for stick insects (say 'fas-mids')*

Instructions

Sam's Hobby Club

Week 6: Make a Stick Puppet

Follow these instructions to make a super stick puppet!

What you need
- a clean polystyrene food tray
- scissors
- a thin stick
- felt tip or gel pens
- some sticky tape
- glue
- some wool or felt
- beads, buttons, etc. for extra decoration
- stick-on googly eyes (optional)

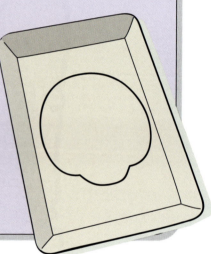

What to do

1. Decide what puppet you want to make – it could be a person, an animal or a fantasy creature. Draw the outline of your puppet on the flat part of the tray. (See diagram.)

2. Carefully cut out the puppet shape. If you are not sure about using scissors, ask an adult to help.

③ Draw on the details such as the eyes, nose and mouth. Stick on the eyes, if you are using them.

④ Stick on some pieces of wool or felt for the hair (or fur or whiskers!)

⑤ Use the beads, buttons, etc. to decorate the puppet. Tape the stick to the back.

And your first stick puppet is ready to have fun! Try making some different characters. You could make up a story about them and put on a play. Send us a photo of your puppet – or your puppet play. We'll put some of the best ones on our Letters Page next month!

Hopscotch

Hopscotch was a very popular game in Victorian times – and it still is! There are several different versions of the rules. Here is one.

What you need
- a flat surface outside that you can draw on
- a piece of chalk
- a flat stone to use as a marker

What to do

1. Draw the hopscotch board on the ground with the piece of chalk.
2. Throw the marker onto square 1.
3. Hop over that square and land with one foot on square 2 and the other on square 3.
4. Hopscotch to the top. This means you hop on one foot on the single squares and jump down on both feet on the double ones.
5. When you get to square 10, hop around to face the start, then hopscotch back. When you reach squares 2 and 3, pick up the marker.
6. Hop over square 1 to the start but do not land on square 1.
7. Throw the marker onto square 2.

8 Repeat instructions 3 to 6, but this time you have to hopscotch without landing on square 2.

9 Keep going until you have thrown the marker to all the numbers. It can be quite hard to throw it into the squares that are further away!

10 If you fall over or wobble off a square, you must go back and do that square again.

You can also play hopscotch with a friend – and this is harder!

You will need two stones as markers.

Take turns to hopscotch, following the same instructions. In this game, however, you have to hopscotch over both markers.

If your marker misses the correct square, or if your foot goes over one of the lines, it is the end of your turn.

Why don't you have a go?

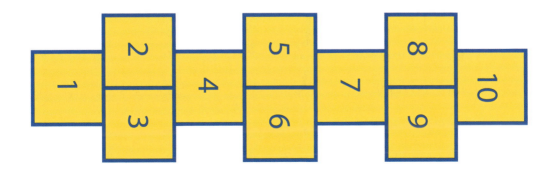

How to Find the Goblin's Gold

What you need
- a spade
- the map
- good weather

What to do

1. Wait until just before midday on May 1st.
2. Leave the house by the back door and go down the garden path.
3. Walk towards the orchard.
4. Wait by the apple tree until exactly midday. (If the sun is not shining you will have to try again next year.)

5. Walk along the shadow of the tree. This will take you into the field next to the orchard.

6. Stop when you get to the end of the shadow.

7. Take seven paces to the right. Turn right and then take another seven paces.

8. Wait until the shadow of a raven passes over the grass in front of you.

9. Dig where the shadow passes and you will find the goblin's gold.

Be careful how you carry it away. The goblin will be on the lookout!

How to Snare the Dragon

Important information for the people of Little Ambleton

What you need
- about ten small animals (they will not be harmed)
- still-as-a-statue potion
- several spades
- a large net with a drawstring around the edge
- a fire extinguisher – or, better still, the fire brigade

What to do

- Meet at 8 p.m. by the well – the dragon is always out hunting then.

- Dig a large pit a few paces in front of the dragon's cave.
- Line the pit with the net.

- Place branches and leaves over the top of the pit so that no one can see it is there.
- Lead the drawstring back into the trees, and cover it with leaves so it cannot be seen.
- Put the animals at the side of the pit nearest the cave. Give them some of the still-as-a-statue potion so they cannot move.
- Hold onto the drawstring and hide among the trees.
- When the dragon comes back, he will try to pounce on the animals and will fall into the pit. When he is in, pull the drawstring tight.

- Put out his fire with the fire extinguisher (or send in the fire brigade).

- Throw the dragon over the cliff.

Invite everyone to a party. The town will be safe at last!

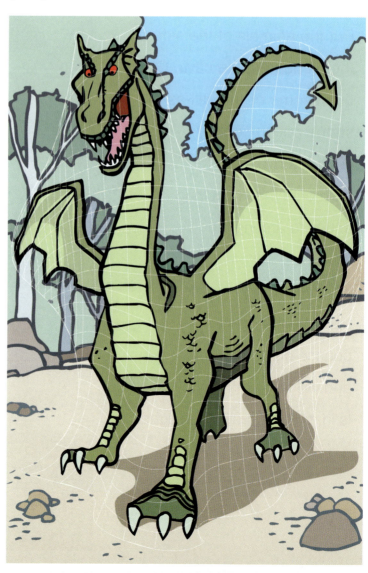

An ABC of Getting About

Aeroplane   An aeroplane is a vehicle with wings and an engine. It flies through the air.

Automobile   An automobile is a motor car. When the automobile was first invented, it was called a *'horseless carriage'*.

Barge   A barge is a long, flat-bottomed boat used on canals and rivers. Barges used to be pulled by horses walking along a path beside the waterway.

Bicycle   A bicycle is a vehicle with two wheels which are held in a frame. The rider moves it along by pushing pedals with their feet. There are other kinds of cycles, for example the *unicycle* and the *tricycle*.

Bus   A bus is a large vehicle for carrying many people. The word 'bus' is short for 'omnibus'. The first omnibus, in London in 1829, was horse-drawn. Buses can be single- or double-decker.

Canoe   A canoe is a small, narrow boat with pointed ends. It moves along by the person or people inside using one or more paddles.

Cart (1) A cart is a vehicle with two or four wheels, pulled by a person or animal and used to carry loads. (2) A cart is a vehicle for carrying people, pulled by one or more horses.

Catamaran A catamaran is a boat which has two **hulls**.

Cruise liner A cruise liner is a very large ship used for holidays at sea. People live on the ship, which stops at different places on the voyage.

Galleon A galleon is a large Spanish sailing ship which was used in the 16th and 17th centuries.

Glider A glider is an *aeroplane* without an engine.

Gondola A gondola is a flat-bottomed boat with high pointed ends, used on the canals in Venice. The boatman stands at the **stern** and pushes it along with one oar.

Hang-glider A hang-glider is a large kite with which a person can glide through the air.

Hansom cab A hansom cab is a two-wheeled horse-drawn carriage. It was the 19th-century version of a *taxi*. Two passengers could sit inside and the driver sat behind.

Horseless carriage — 'Horseless carriage' was the name given to the first *automobiles* at the end of the 19th century. At the time, most road vehicles were pulled by horses, but the automobile had an engine to drive it along.

Hydrofoil — A hydrofoil is a boat with a special **hull** that skims over the water. This helps it to go faster.

Kayak — A kayak is a small one-person *canoe*. It has a covering that fits around the canoeist's waist.

Lifeboat — A lifeboat is a boat used for rescuing people at sea.

Lorry — A lorry is a large vehicle usually used for carrying goods.

Pedalo — A pedalo is a pleasure boat driven by a person pushing pedals.

Punt — A punt is a flat-bottomed boat which is square at both ends. A person stands at one end and moves it along using a pole to push against the river bed.

Quinquereme — A quinquereme is a boat with five lines of oarsmen on each side. Boats like this were used by the Romans and Greeks. The oarsmen were often slaves or criminals.

Raft	A raft is a flat, floating structure which can be used as a boat.
Rickshaw	A rickshaw is a two-wheeled carriage pulled by one or more people. They often have hoods to keep passengers dry.
Rowing boat	A rowing boat is a boat that is moved along by oars.
Sedan chair	A sedan chair is a chair within which someone is carried. People called porters lift the chair on long poles. In the 17th and 18th centuries people used them to be carried through the streets.
Sleigh	Sleigh is another word for a large sledge. It is a vehicle on runners for carrying people or goods over snow and ice. It can be pulled by people, horses, dogs or reindeer.
Spacecraft	A spacecraft is a vehicle with a rocket engine which can travel in outer space.
Stilts	Stilts are poles with supports for the feet. Using a pair of stilts, someone can walk lifted above the ground. They are often used for street entertainment or in circuses.

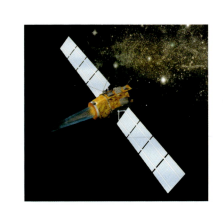

Submarine   A submarine is a vessel that can travel under the water.

Taxi   A taxi is a car which carries passengers who pay for the journey. The amount to be paid is usually shown on a meter.

Train   A train is a line of carriages or trucks pulled by an engine along a railway. Trains can carry goods or passengers.

Tram   A tram is a large vehicle for carrying passengers. It is similar to a *bus*, except that it runs along rails on the road and is powered by electricity.

Tricycle   A tricycle is a cycle with three wheels – one at the front and two at the back.

Underground   The underground is a railway that runs through tunnels under the streets. There are undergrounds in many cities in the world. The one in London is also called 'the tube'.

Unicycle   A unicycle is a cycle with one wheel. It is used for tricks and entertainment.

hull – *the frame of a boat*
stern – *the back of a boat*

Letter from Mr Gruff to Mrs Washer

The Looking Glass Primary School

Warren Lane

Wonderland

8th April 2005

Dear Mrs Washer

I am writing to you to complain about the behaviour of your son Jack.

First of all, I am cross because he is probably the laziest child that I have ever met. He has not yet finished any of his homework and it is always handed in late. He is idle in class and never seems to know any of the answers.

Secondly, it is dreadful that he does not pay attention during lessons. As a result he does not yet know the letters of the alphabet, he cannot add up simple sums and he spends all the lesson time day-dreaming about castles in the air. Sometimes, he puts his head down on his arms and within five minutes he is snoring. Does he get enough sleep at night?

Thirdly, I am concerned that he has been telling the most extraordinary lies to the other children. He claims that he sold your old cow, Milky-white, for a few beans. I know that he is not a very bright boy but surely he has not sold your cow for a handful of beans? He has been telling the children that they are magic beans.

However, I was sorry to hear that after school last week Jack hurt his head. He claims that he was trying to fetch some water and he slipped.

I would appreciate it if you could come up to the school so that we could talk over these issues.

Yours sincerely

Mr Gruff
Headteacher

Letter from Jack to Jill

Bushytail Cottage
Rabbit Avenue
Wonderland
14th April 2005

Dear Jill

I thought I would let you know what has been happening in the village.

Last week, our old cow Milky-white stopped giving milk. So, my mum asked me to take her to the market and sell her. On the way, I met an old man who swapped the cow for some strange-looking beans. The old man told me that the beans were magic.

When I arrived home, my mum was not pleased. She threw the beans out of the window and sent me to bed with no supper.

The next morning, when I woke up my room was strangely dark and shady. As soon as I got outside I could see why. The beans had grown into a giant beanstalk that went up and up till it reached the sky!

Later that day, I climbed out of my bedroom window onto the stalk. It was made like a big plaited ladder. Next, I climbed up and up till

I reached the top.

After a while, I came to a huge castle where I met the wife of a giant. She was very kind to me and fed me a hunk of bread and cheese and a jug of milk.

Just at that moment, the giant returned, so his wife hid me in the oven. Immediately, he started sniffing and sniffing as if he could smell me!

After that, his wife fed him breakfast. Then he got out three sacks of gold and began counting his money. Soon he fell fast asleep, so I crept out of the oven and stole one of the bags!

Finally, I climbed back down the beanstalk with the gold. You should have seen my old ma when I showed her the golden coins!

I hope you get well soon. My head is much better.

Luv
Jack

Letter from Henny Penny to Jack

Henny Penny's Pet Shop

By the Crooked Stile

Wonderland

24th April 2005

Dear Jack

Thank you for your recent letter asking for information about keeping golden hens. Golden creatures are very rare and hard to look after. It is not always easy to keep golden hens or geese, but I will try to explain how to do it.

First, you will need to make sure that your hen is kept in a clean and tidy pen. This should provide enough room for the hen to run around and scratch in safety. You have to make sure that foxes and wolves cannot enter because there is nothing tastier to a fox than golden hen or goose!

It is important to make sure that golden hens have the correct food. They will need to eat a regular diet of the finest corn because their stomachs are delicate. The three little pigs do sell excellent corn that comes recommended.

When your hen is tired, you should make sure that it gets plenty of sleep. A tired hen will not lay well. If a golden hen or goose does not get enough sleep, then the owner must expect that the eggs will be made of silver or copper.

Also, golden hens need plenty of water to drink so that they do not become thirsty. A thirsty hen will only lay marble eggs.

Do not talk unkindly to your hen. This will cause it to sulk. An unhappy hen will refuse to talk and will never lay eggs of any type.

I do hope that the above explanation will be of help. Do give my best wishes to your mother. I hope that your golden hen lays happily for many years.

Yours sincerely
Henny Penny

Letter from Contrary Mary to Jack Washer

Silver Bell Cottage

Rabbit Avenue

Wonderland

27th April 2005

Dear Jack Washer

I am writing to you to congratulate you on your latest daring adventure.

First, I was so thrilled to find that I had a magic beanstalk growing in the garden next door to me. It has brought me so much pleasure.

Next, I was delighted to hear that you had come into some good fortune by exploring the sky lands above. I was amazed to hear not only that you had climbed up the stalk once but that you had returned on two other occasions. You are such a daring and courageous boy. The whole neighbourhood is proud of you.

Also, it has been a real pleasure to live next door to someone who takes the care of his livestock so seriously. Your golden hen has the most impressive pen and is so well fed that it has cheered up my little red hen no end.

After that, I was astonished to return home last week and find that the beanstalk had been cut right down. What a clever boy you are and a credit to your mother! Everyone is delighted that you have defeated the ugly brute. The one thing that we did not need in the town was an ogre or a giant living nearby. They are so troublesome and inconvenient!

Finally, since you took up the harp, my garden has been full of music from dawn to dusk.
I have especially enjoyed the way the harp sings in the middle of the night and helps to while away the dark hours.

Well done again and do please pass on my best wishes to your mother.

Yours sincerely

Contrary Mary

Extracts from Four Letters

The Looking Glass Primary School

Warren Lane

Wonderland

8th April 2005

Dear Mrs Washer

I am writing to you to complain about the behaviour of your son Jack.

Bushytail Cottage

Rabbit Avenue

Wonderland

14th April 2005

Dear Jill

I thought I would let you know what has been happening in the village.

Henny Penny's Pet Shop

By the Crooked Stile

Wonderland

24th April 2005

Dear Jack

Thank you for your recent letter asking for information about keeping golden hens. Golden creatures are very rare and hard to look after.

Silver Bell Cottage

Rabbit Avenue

Wonderland

27th April 2005

Dear Jack Washer

I am writing to you to congratulate you on your latest daring adventure.

An Invitation to the Ball

The Great Summer Palace

On the Hill

Great Swankyshire

24th July 2005

The Hardup Family are all invited by His Royal Highness the King to attend a fabulous Summer Ball

at the Great Summer Palace

on Saturday next,

July 31st 2005

The Great Summer Ball will begin at 8 o'clock.

Carriages must arrive to take you home no later than 1 o'clock.

Gentlemen should wear the finest clothes and powdered wigs. Swords and pistols must be left at home.

Ladies must wear ball gowns and tiaras or fancy hats.

There will dancing all evening to the wonderful music of

Monsieur Mouse and his Mini Micekins. They will play all your favourite waltzes and courtly dances.

The King has decreed that the Great Summer Ball will have a theme of animals. Therefore, in accordance with His Majesty's wishes, animal masks must be worn.

Please find enclosed details of the menu. If you are a vegetarian or need special food, inform the cook, Miss Hubbard. The great feast will feature the creations of Gordon Ram and Madame Sheep.

Also attached are directions to the palace.

R.S.V.P. to the Prince Charm, A.S.A.P.

T.T.F.N.

Directions to the Great Summer Ball

Please pass on these instructions to your coach driver. In the past, many people have become lost on their way to the King's Great Summer Palace. If you become lost, do not leave your carriage:

in the forest – there are wolves;

in the mountains – there are ogres;

by the river – there is a troll under the bridge;

by Jack's beanstalk – a giant lives on top of the stalk!

Letter from Loolabell Hardup to Mistress Simkins

The Great Hardup Hall
Piper's Lane
Swankyshire
26th July 2005

Dear Mistress Simkins

My sister and I have been invited to attend the Great Summer Ball at the King's Palace next weekend. We are writing to ask if you would be able to create a pair of the most beautiful ball gowns for us to wear.

Would it be possible for Leticia to be dressed in lime green, with a luminous pattern that wobbles as she moves? She would like to make sure that everyone notices her. She would also like to have a large floral hat.

Could you arrange for me to be dressed more beautifully than my sister? I certainly do not want her to outshine me. So, I would like to wear a bright red and yellow striped gown with a large Christmas tree on top. Could this please have a flashing set of lights? That way the Prince is bound to notice me coming.

Can we visit you to be measured on Wednesday morning? May we visit to try on the gowns on Friday? That will give a little time for any adjustments.

Yours demandingly

Loolabell Hardup

P.S. If that pesky little wretch Cinderella tries to get a gown, give her a flea in the ear and send her running home.

Letter from Cinders to Buttons

The Great Hardup Hall

Piper's Lane

Swankyshire

28th July 2005

Dear Buttons

I am writing to tell you all about what has been happening at home.

Last month, my father got married again while he was away on his trip to America.

When he returned to Hardup Hall, he brought with him his new wife and her two daughters.

At first, I was very excited because I thought that we would be one big happy family. However, that was not to be. I think my stepmother must hate me because she makes me do all the cleaning, washing and cooking. I work myself to the bone all day long while my two sisters do not lift a finger. They just shout at me and boss me about. They are the PITS.

Last weekend, we received a letter from the King inviting us all to a Great Summer Ball. Of course, my sisters are allowed to go and are having new ball gowns made for them. I am not allowed to go and have to stay at home. I must polish the pots and pans.

Yesterday was a dreadful day because they locked me in the kitchen all morning. They went out to the dressmaker's. All I had for company was the family of mice and their ratty chums who live in the walls. They are very friendly. Some of them eat scraps of bread and cheese from my hand.

This morning, I noticed that when the postman called, my sisters grabbed all the letters. Well, I managed to sneak one away while they were not looking. It was a letter from my fairy godmother. It seems that she has been sending me presents and I have not been getting them. Do you think that the sisters have been stealing them?

Finally, I have decided that I will go to the Great Summer Ball – one way or another. Even if I have to go in a gown made of tattered rags. I wish that you were with me and I hope that you are keeping well.

Lots of love

Cinders
xxx

Letter from the Lord Chamberlain

The Palace, On the Hill, Great Swankyshire

5th August 2005

Dear House Owner

The King has asked me to write to all loyal subjects to tell them about recent events. This is a matter of the utmost importance.

It has been drawn to the King's attention that at the Great Summer Ball his son, the young Prince Charm, spent the whole evening in the company of the most delightful and beautiful young lady. As the lady wore the most original cat mask, she remained unrecognised by any person. The prince was obviously much enamoured with the young lady.

However, when midnight struck, the strangest incident occurred. The young lady in question departed from the Prince in great haste. She left the dance floor and dashed down the steps to her coach. The coach sped away into the night as the last sound of the midnight bell echoed.

Once again, the coach has not been recognised by anyone. It has been reported to the King that the footmen were whiskery and the horses rather unusual in appearance. Furthermore, the coach must have been made in another land because it was more like a pumpkin on wheels than a coach.

The Prince has taken to his bed since the event and will not speak to anyone. His Majesty's doctors say that he is suffering from an especially bad attack of lovesickness. The only cure will be finding this young girl.

As she fled the palace, the young girl's slipper fell off. It is made of some sort of glass or finely crafted crystal.

In order to find the girl, the King has asked the Prince and his guards to visit all the houses in the town. Every girl of marriageable age should be made available so that each one can try on the slipper to see if it fits.

The Prince will call at your house on the 10th August. I trust that you will comply with this order.

The Lord Chamberlain
By order of the King